Children
of the Black Skirt

Angela Betzien

Currency Press, Sydney

CURRENCY TEENAGE SERIES

First published in 2005
by Currency Press Pty Ltd,
PO Box 2287, Strawberry Hills, NSW, 2012, Australia
enquiries@currency.com.au
www.currency.com.au

NATIONAL LIBRARY OF AUSTRALIA CIP DATA

Betzien, Angela, 1978–.
Children of the black skirt.
ISBN 0 86819 760 2.
I. Title. (Series: Currency teenage series).
A822.4

Publication of this title was assisted
by the Commonwealth Government
through the Australia Council, its
arts funding and advisory body.

Contents

Set for Currency Press by Dean Nottle
Printed by Hyde Park Press, Richmond, South Australia.
Cover design by Kate Florance
Cover photograph by Stephen Henry.

REALtv is an artistic team that formed in late 2000. They have created new work for Queensland Theatre Company (*The Orphanage Project*, 2003), La Boite Theatre (*Kingswood Kids*, 2003), Queensland Arts Council (*Children of the Black Skirt*) and QPAQ's Stage X festival (*The Suitcase*, 2001). Real TV has received grants from Arts Queensland (2002 and 2001) and the Australia Council (2002). *Children of the Black Skirt* is Real TV's seminal work and has toured with Queensland Arts Council to Queensland regional and metropolitan high schools. The popularity of the play resulted in a second regional tour of Queensland in 2004 and a subsequent tour throughout regional Victoria presented by Regional Arts Victoria. In 2005 the play tours South Australia, as part of Adelaide's Come Out Festival for Young People, to Regional Victoria, and the work will also have a season at the Sydney Opera House as part of the HouseEd program. Real TV has received numerous awards for their productions. Real TV's mission is to produce quality theatrical Australian stories.

From left, above: Pete Goodwin, Angela Betzien, Leticia Cáceres; below, the 2004 touring cast: Louise Brehmer, Jodie Le Vesconte, Janine Mattews.

Children of the Black Skirt was developed by Real TV and produced by Queensland Arts Council. It first toured in 2003, throughout regional and metropolitan Queensland high schools with the following cast:

Jodie Le Vesconte	Black Skirt / Harrold Horrocks
Louise Brehmer	New One
Sandy Greenwood	Old One / Rosie

Director, Leticia Cáceres
Composer & Sound Designer, Pete Goodwin
Designer, Tanja Beer

The play toured again in 2004 with the following cast:

Jodie Le Vesconte	Black Skirt / Harrold Horrocks
Louise Brehmer	New One
Janine Mattews	Old One / Rosie

The play is dedicated to children who have lived in institutions.

Acknowledgements

Helen Strube, Libby Anstis, Toni Postans, Erin Milne, Louise Brehmer, Adrianne Jones, Annie Roylance, Michael Gow, Kathryn Kelly, Linda Page, Fiona Doyle, Sandy Greenwood, Jodie Le Vesconte, Laurel Collins, Janine Matthews, Cheryl Buchanan, Queensland Theatre Company, La Boite Theatre, Kyas Sheriff, Helen Weder, Michael Kaempff, Rockhampton City Council, Judy Couttie, Rockhampton Dreamtime Cultural Centre, Bob Blair, Anthony Pirovich, Stephen Henry, Tanja Beer, Jody Betzien, Jim Lawson, Drama Victoria, Kurt Luthy, the Cáceres family, Glenala State High School, Samantha Betzien, Regional Arts Victoria, Queensland Arts Council, Queensland Government through the Department of Education and the Arts.

Photographs by Stephen Henry; copyright © Stephen Henry & Real TV 2004.

arts access statewide...

For further information about Real TV, or to purchase the *Children of the Black Skirt* music and sound on compact disc, contact: www.realtv.net.au.

A Project History

In September 2001 Real TV (Angela Betzien, Pete Goodwin and myself) was approached by Queensland Arts Council (QAC) and asked to create a new work for young people. QAC had been attracted to Real TV because of our reputation for creating theatrically exciting and accessible, political plays. Our brief was to create a challenging work for upper primary and high school, which addressed the curriculum.

This invitation was a great honour for Real TV. QAC recognised the importance of collaborating with artistic teams, breaking with the traditional commissioning model of working solely with a writer. The brief was also very appealing to Real TV because the possibilities for the work were endless.

It was late one evening, at the back of the Cement Box Theatre where Real TV was presenting its fourth work (*Princess of Suburbia*) that the idea emerged to explore the topic of orphanages. Angela had had some early experiences with orphanages in her childhood, having attended a number of religious education camps at an old orphanage outside her hometown. Everyone was excited by the potential of this subject matter in terms of its political issues and theatrical possibilities.

From that night onwards, Real TV began a rigourous campaign planning the project and researching the subject matter. The team also started brainstorming different non-naturalistic styles of performance that could be used to tell what was panning out to be a very dark and Gothic piece of theatre. It was envisaged that two creative development phases throughout 2002 would be required for this work to take shape.

The Real TV team and actors Laurel Collins, Jodie Le Vesconte and Kyas Sherriff embarked on a week-long expedition to Central Queensland. We spent a day at the orphanage Angela had visited as a child. This experience gave everyone the chance to experience the area's unique aural, physical, cultural and historical landscape.

There were also very long and intensive discussions about the history of Australia, the treatment of Indigenous people since invasion, the link between institutionalisation and cultural genocide and the culture of silence and cover-up by government agencies and religious institutions. The outcome of this process was the development of a strong ensemble of artists; a common understanding about the project, its themes and vision; and a wealth of sense memory experiences from which the actors could draw. The major dramatic question for the work emerged: how does the treatment of children reflect our society and shape future generations?

Between April and July, Angela wrote the first draft. We soon realised the work was too dark for young audiences. We faced a major dilemma: how do we tell stories about the most painful cases of child abuse in a play that is appropriate for young audiences?

Real TV, plus designer Tanja Beer and the original three actors spent two weeks working on the first draft of the script. This phase gave everyone the opportunity to work out the logistics of the script, its structure, narratives, characters and theatrical demands. At this point we realised that by drawing on fairytale traditions and styles we could communicate dark subject matter metaphorically.

An audience of high school students, industry and the general public were invited to view this work in progress and respond through feedback forms. Much of this feedback was extremely positive and these responses formed the basis for Angela's subsequent draft of the script in preparation for production.

By February 2003, Angela had completed a production draft of the script for the first tour of *Children of the Black Skirt*. The show was rehearsed over the course of nine days. The biggest challenge of this process was in defining the conventions of the work. For example, the sheets became an integral part of the spirit sequences, creating character and context for these stories as well signifying the release of the spirits at the end of each account. Another stumbling block was how to transform the Black Skirt into Harrold Horrocks in front of the audience.

The actors returned from the first tour of Queensland loaded with feedback from teachers and students. A redraft of the script took place in time for the tour in 2004. A new final story was added, that of the Black Skirt's baby, which clarified much of the mystery surrounding the character.

Over the last two years of touring, we have received some wonderful responses from young people and teachers about the play. Many have told us that *Children of the Black Skirt* is the best piece of theatre they've ever seen. This is a heartening affirmation that disputes the cynical perception of young people as politically and socially apathetic. Young audiences have also been stunned into silence by the ominous Black Skirt. They have expressed their genuine fear of this character whose presence is created without special effects, through the superb physical skills of the actor. As theatre makers who believe wholeheartedly in the power of this medium, this is more than enough encouragement to continue to create engaging theatre for young people.

In the meantime Real TV hopes that *Children of the Black Skirt* will haunt and enchant people across Australia and, one day, around the world, for years to come.

Leticia Cáceres
(Director, premiere Real TV production)
January 2005

Composer's Notes

For the original touring production I drew inspiration for the musical score from the records my family owned when I was a child. These included old recordings of Australian colonial folk songs that my dad bought in his 20s prior to being married, as well as classic children's records including Patsy Biscoe, songs from Sesame Street, and the Walt Disney Little Golden Book series. The scratchiness and crackle reminiscent of these records was deliberately kept in the soundtrack to evoke a sense of nostalgia.

In a manner much more akin to film than theatre, a complex layer of sound and sound effects was added to the music to help create the foreboding presence of the orphanage itself, as well as the unique, eerie mood of the Australian landscape. The sound of the spirits of dead children who come to haunt the orphanage at night were created from sampling the actors' voices into a computer and electronically manipulating the pitch and timbre of their voices to sound like children.

In performance, the music and sound were operated by the three actors from a minidisc player concealed backstage.

Pete Goodwin
(Composer, premiere Real TV production)

Above: Setting up.
Below: The touring set.

Setting

Children of the Black Skirt was written specifically for schools touring and therefore the set was designed very simply to ensure it was transportable and easily assembled by three actors in any classroom context.

Major set and prop items include the following:

  Two small wooden dormitory beds
  Twelve sheets
  Two pillows
  Two wooden boxes
  A calico backdrop with a gauze window
  A wire clothesline
  A washing basket
  A small suitcase (inside the suitcase is an item of underwear, a teddy bear, a book of fairytales)
  Several wooden 'Dolly' pegs (including those used to create The Black Skirt and Harrold Horrocks puppets)
  A teacup and saucer and a serving tray
  A scrubbing brush
  A set of keys
  A large pair of scissors
  A sound system
  Five costumes (New One, Old One, The Black Skirt, Harrold Horrocks and Rosie)

The intention is that actors will utilise the basic set items of sheets, pegs and pillows in multiple ways to create character and context. For example, sheets might be hung to create the appearance of a forest in Maggie's story, or a pillow used to play the baby in Lizzie's story.

In the original production of the play, the sheets were used to symbolise the spirits. The spirits are 'released' from their orphanage world when the sheet is flung out into the air.

Production Notes

The play was originally intended for performance by three female actors playing multiple roles, however it is also suited to a larger ensemble of actors. An entire class could be enrolled as orphanage children and the multiple roles distributed among the group. Although the play has been performed by a cast of three females, the work could easily be adapted for an all-male or a gender-mixed cast.

In many cases, stage directions have not been prescribed, however, whenever possible actors should physicalise the action in the stories. There is also flexibility within the text to creatively explore the various 'orphanage sequences'. For example, 'morning dormitory routines' or 'work routines' can be choreographed sequences that might employ the ensemble's dance and/or physical performance skills. Similarly, there is also opportunity to create live soundscapes instead of pre-recording.

The sequence in which the letters of the orphanage children are recited could be extended to include letters that students have written themselves. Similarly, students might like to write or improvise the story of a present day spirit. This will encourage young people to consider the contemporary relevance of the historical themes and issues in the play.

Transformation of character

The text requires the actor to transform characters. In the touring production of the play, these transformations always occurred in front of the audience. In accordance with Brechtian alienation techniques this theatrical convention is employed to challenge naturalistic modes of performance and engage audiences with the politics of character.

If the text is performed by three actors, doubling of the main characters is also required. For example, New One/Rosie and The Black Skirt/ Harrold Horrocks. These transformations provide a challenge to the creative team and should be solved with theatricality and imagination.

Characters

Lost Bush Children (3)

New One, eight years old, new arrival at the orphanage (The identity number J78 is worn on New One's uniform. The J represents her junior status in the orphanage.)

Old One, eleven years old, Aboriginal child at the orphanage. (The identity number S78 is worn on Old One's uniform. The S represents her senior status. Senior children share an identity number with Junior children for whom they have a responsibility of care.)

The Black Skirt or **Miss Emily Greenant**, the silent Governess of the orphanage

Rosie, the Aboriginal laundry woman

John, Cockney chimney sweep, 1790s

Lizzie, Scottish girl, 1850s

Maggie, Australian girl living on the frontier, 1880s

Lucy, Aboriginal 'domestic' girl, 1910s

Harrold Horrocks, Inspector of Orphanages

Iris, Australian girl living in the city slums, 1930s

Tom, boy from Yorkshire, 1940s

Ruby, Aboriginal girl living in the city, 1960s

Baby, stillborn, 1890s

Gentleman, Banker, Beggar, Magistrate, 1790s

Lizzie's Mother, 1850s

Maggie's Mother, Father, 1880s

Nun, Mrs Connell, 1910s

Iris's Dad, Landlord, Neighbour, 1930s

Fat Man, Tom's Mother, 1940s

Ruby's Mum, Welfare, 1960s

The Black Skirt's Aunt, Doctor, 1890s

These characters can be played by three actors.
Suggested doubles for main characters are:
Rosie / New One; Black Skirt / Harrold Horrocks

Above: Discovering the Victorian dress.
Below: The sound of a train.

An abandoned orphanage somewhere in the Australian landscape.

Three CHILDREN emerge from the bush. They are lost. They are barefoot and their clothes are dirty and torn.

As the CHILDREN encounter the orphanage they fall silent. Warily at first, they begin to explore. They pick up old scrubbing brushes, overturn dormitory beds with their dusty sheets, and peer into cobwebbed suitcases and boxes.

One of the CHILDREN discovers a very old Victorian-style black dress lying on the floor. She shows the others, who dare her to try it on. Attached to the black dress is an enormous pair of scissors. The other two children also find dresses and try them on. They giggle at the game of dress-up.

As the child draws the black dress over her own clothes, she suddenly becomes the character who once owned the dress, the cruel governess of the orphanage, known by all as THE BLACK SKIRT.

The other children, as if trapped in this strange spell, also become the characters who once owned the dresses they now wear…

One girl becomes the character of ROSIE, the Aboriginal laundry woman who worked at the orphanage.

The other child becomes NEW ONE, a new arrival at the orphanage.

The sound of a train.

NEW ONE picks up a small suitcase and sits. She begins to move with the rhythm of a train.

The train comes to a halt and NEW ONE is greeted by ROSIE who takes her suitcase and leads her through the orphanage to the shower room.

The sound of dripping water.

Rosie Listen now, this is what yer do. Yer take all yer things off, that's right. Yer got to wash yerself real well, then put these on. These are all yer things. These are the things yer wear at night 'n these are the things yer wear at day. Yer understand? That lady in the black skirt gets cross if yer do the wrong thing. You gotta do what she tells yer, everythin' she tells yer. Hush now, don't cry, hush now.

ROSIE leaves.

NEW ONE is left to whimper in the dark.

ROSIE presents NEW ONE's suitcase to THE BLACK SKIRT.

THE BLACK SKIRT opens the suitcase and silently inspects its contents. She withdraws, one by one, an item of underwear, a teddy bear, a book of fairytales.

She's eight, Missus. Her mother 'n father is dead, Missus, she's a Ward of the State, Missus. Yes, Missus, I'll burn them things, Missus. No, Missus. Do what you say, Missus.

THE BLACK SKIRT places these items back in the suitcase and returns it to ROSIE. THE BLACK SKIRT leaves.

ROSIE goes to the incinerator in the orphanage grounds. She sings as she regretfully burns the contents of NEW ONE's suitcase. At the last moment, ROSIE spares NEW ONE's book of fairytales and hides it in her washing basket. ROSIE hurries away.

THE BLACK SKIRT appears in the shower room carrying a heavy set of keys. She leads NEW ONE through the dark corridors of the orphanage to the girls' dormitory, then silently instructs her where she is to sleep.

THE BLACK SKIRT leaves the dormitory.

OLD ONE, a young Aboriginal girl, is kneeling by her bed in prayer. She quickly finishes, then jumps into bed.

NEW ONE begins to cry.

OLD ONE withdraws a candle and a box of matches hidden beneath her bed. She lights a match, then the candle. The light startles NEW ONE into silence.

Old One It's all right New One, hop into bed. Quick, before she comes back.

NEW ONE gets into her bed. OLD ONE blows out the candle.

The ghostly sound of a baby crying.

THE BLACK SKIRT can be seen nursing what appears to be a baby in the distant corridors of the orphanage.

The voices of spirit children fill the orphanage. They are the ghosts of Children Past.

NEW ONE covers her head with her bed sheet. She is terrified.

OLD ONE is familiar with the spirits. She tosses and turns in her bed, annoyed that she can't sleep for all the noise they are making.

The spirit voices fade as the sound of a kookaburra heralds the morning.

OLD ONE addresses the audience.

Hey, all you girls. New One looks like she's heard a ghost. You have. Them the spirits. Them the sad lil' fellas come here every night. Look, all you girls, New One so scared she peed the bed. Don't worry, them spirits won't hurt yer. Them just kids like us.

THE BLACK SKIRT enters the dormitory. OLD ONE warns NEW ONE to keep her head down. THE BLACK SKIRT claps once. OLD ONE jumps out of her bed and kneels on the floor in prayer. NEW ONE tries to follow OLD ONE's lead.

This is our Home,
Let Love abide here.
Let us always speak the Truth,
Love the Truth,
And live the Truth.
May contentment dwell in our hearts,
May our Home be a place of joy and companionship
Where the love of our Matron reigns.
In the name of her we pray.
Amen.

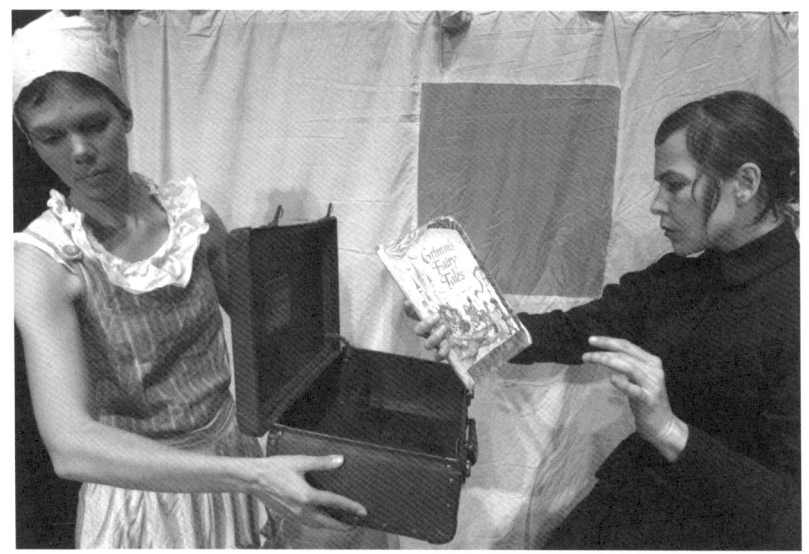

Above: Black Skirt opens the suitcase.
Below: The spirits come.

THE BLACK SKIRT claps again and the children make their beds. THE BLACK SKIRT inspects the beds. She discovers a wet sheet on NEW ONE's bed, picks it up and covers NEW ONE's head with it. THE BLACK SKIRT claps again and OLD ONE leads the chant of humiliation...

Pee the beds, pee the beds, pee the beds...

THE BLACK SKIRT sends NEW ONE out into the orphanage grounds where she is forced to march back and forth chanting...

New One   Pee the beds, pee the beds, pee the beds...

ROSIE appears in the dormitory, THE BLACK SKIRT passes her.

Rosie   Them kids pee the beds again, Missus? Yeah, I'll wash them sheets, Missus. You send them lil' ones to me, I'll fix 'em up. Yes, Missus. No talkin' to them lil' ones, I know, Missus. Yes, Missus. Do what you say, Missus.

ROSIE picks up her wash basket, goes to the clothesline in the orphanage grounds and begins to hang sheets on the line.

NEW ONE appears near the washing line still wearing the sheet on her head. She sees ROSIE and watches her from a distance.

A curlew calls and the ghostly sound of a baby crying echoes through the landscape.

The sound of the children's spirit voices in the wind.

ROSIE hears these spirits and soothes them by singing an Aboriginal lullaby.

The spirit voices fade.

ROSIE notices NEW ONE and beckons her over. She takes the wet sheet from NEW ONE's head and gives her another clean folded one.

That song keeps them spirits quiet. Don't want 'em too big, they tear them sheets off the line. Dunno where I learned that, jus' know it. Them spirits like tellin' stories too. You like stories?

ROSIE gives NEW ONE her book of fairytales that she saved from the incinerator. She sees THE BLACK SKIRT approaching.

Keep that hid, yer hear. Best go now. Quick.

NEW ONE hides the book under her clean sheet and runs inside the orphanage. ROSIE gathers up her wash basket and hurries off to work.

NEW ONE returns to the dormitory, hiding her book of fairytales beneath her pillow.

THE BLACK SKIRT claps and the orphanage children assemble to sing 'God Save the Queen'.

The song ends and the children queue for dinner. They are served by THE BLACK SKIRT. The meal quickly disappears, but the children are still hungry. NEW ONE is about to ask for more but OLD ONE quickly hushes her.

THE BLACK SKIRT claps once, dismissing the girls from dinner.

Rosie's lullaby.

The children return to their dormitory. OLD ONE kneels by her bed, NEW ONE joins her. They quickly finish praying and leap into their beds.

Night falls.

The voices of the spirit children fill the orphanage.

Again, NEW ONE is terrified by the strange sounds. OLD ONE can't sleep.

Soon, OLD ONE gets out of her bed.

Old One Can't yer sleep? Them spirits too noisy? You wanna story?

NEW ONE shows OLD ONE the fairytale book ROSIE has returned to her.

No, one of them spirit stories?

OLD ONE addresses the audience enrolling them as children in the dormitory.

Dinner.

Come on, you lil' ones, come round here. Come close, that's right.
This is a story 'bout a lil' fella come from far far away.

> *OLD ONE takes on the character of a Cockney English boy from
> the 1790s.*

John I could pick a pocket like no pocket picka could. But one day I
was spotted. And the gentleman said…

> *OLD ONE looks to NEW ONE to play along with the storytelling
> game.*

… and the gentleman said…

> *NEW ONE finds her voice and joins the game, playing the other
> characters in the story. The girls physicalise the action using the
> few objects available to them in the dormitory.*

Gentleman Stop thief!

John And as I ran 'n ran as fast as I could, all down the street, others
joined in…

Banker Stop thief!

John Shouted the fat-faced banker.

Beggar Stop thief!

John Shouted the one-armed beggar hopin' to get some reward.

Voices Stop thief!

John Shouted the butcherer, the baker, the candlestick maker.

Voices Stop thief!

John Shouted the bookseller, the street urchin, the iron monger.
None, not one of 'em could stop me. That was until the
cobblestone, loose at the end of the street, did trip me, and as I
fell, my life fell with me as if I had a noose about me neck.

> *NEW ONE takes on the role of a MAGISTRATE.*

Magistrate Name?

John John Dwyer

Magistrate Age?

John Nine years.

Magistrate Place of birth?

John East London.

Magistrate Height?

John Three foot eleven and a half inches.

Magistrate Complexion?

John Ruddy, freckled and pock-pitted.

Magistrate Hair?

John Brown.

Magistrate Eyes?

John Grey.

Magistrate Education?

John None.

Magistrate Occupation?

John Chimney sweep.

Magistrate You are charged with stealing a purse containing a
    penny from a woman who keeps an apple stall in Hampshire
    Road. How do you plead?

John Not guilty, Sir.

'I ran and ran...'

Above: The Black Skirt's keys.
Below: Lizzie's job.

Magistrate I sentence you to transportation to Australia, seven years hard labour.

John When I reached Australia they stretched me by me scrawny white neck 'til I was dead, dead, dead.

OLD ONE releases the spirit of JOHN from the orphanage by flinging a sheet out into the air.

OLD ONE and NEW ONE return to being themselves. They hear the sound of THE BLACK SKIRT's keys in the hallway and jump into bed.

The ghostly sound of a baby crying.

THE BLACK SKIRT can be seen nursing what appears to be a baby in the distant corridors of the orphanage.

The sound of the baby fades and the spirit voices return.

OLD ONE encourages NEW ONE to lead the storytelling.

NEW ONE listens to the spirits and becomes LIZZIE, a girl from Scotland in the 1850s. This time OLD ONE plays all the other parts.

Lizzie It was my job to look after the bairns. I was never nowhere without a bairn in me arms.

NEW ONE looks around for something to play the baby. OLD ONE tosses NEW ONE a pillow.

I could play any game with a bairn in me arms, Hopscotch 'n Red Rover 'n Egg 'n Spoon races. I could beat any idiot boy at it too.

LIZZIE plays Hopscotch, Red Rover and Egg and Spoon races with the 'baby' in her arms.

OLD ONE becomes HAMISH.

Hamish Why don't yer go home, Lizzie. Yer can't play with a bairn in yer arms. Why don't yer go home 'n be like a girl 'n look after 'em proper?

Lizzie Said Hamish McDonald, who didn't like that I could beat him. I took no notice of 'im. He was a red-faced idiot that smelt like pigs, anyway. One day I did drop the bairn on its head. Hamish McDonald, the red-faced idiot that smelt like pigs, said to me…

Hamish   Look what yer've done, Lizzie. Yer've dropped the bairn on its head. Yer'll have to stop playin' now 'n be a proper lady.

Lizzie   I just picked it up 'n washed its bleedin' head 'n began the game all over. I didn't want to be a lady. But my mother said…

OLD ONE becomes LIZZIE'S MOTHER.

Mother   You must be a good girl, Lizzie, 'n look after the bairns 'n behave like a proper lady or else no one will ever marry yer 'n yer'll be an old maid forever.

Lizzie   But I did hate the thought of bein' a wife and if I were ever to have a bairn of me own I would right away drown it in the washin' water or throw it in the fire or slit its throat with the butter knife 'cos I did hate the bairns so much. Then my mother heard about the ship that was carryin' girls to meet their future husbands in Van Dieman's Land.

Mother   They say there's hundreds of men with gentlemanly ways who own miles and miles of farmland and plenty of cows 'n pigs 'n hens and they are all lonely 'n lookin' for wives.

Lizzie   And I thought, too bad for them. But at thirteen years of age my mother sent me away with the two pounds saved from the matchbox makin'.

Mother   Here's the two pounds saved from the matchbox makin'. Now be on yer wee way 'n make sure yer brush yer hair 'n pinch yer cheeks 'n clean yer teeth 'n straighten yer skirt before yer meet yer future husband in Van Dieman's Land.

LIZZIE'S MOTHER waves her goodbye.

Lizzie   I was never to see my family. Never to see Scotland 'n never, thank the Lord, to see Hamish McDonald, who smelt like pigs anyway, again.

NEW ONE releases the spirit of LIZZIE from the orphanage by flinging a sheet out into the air.

Again NEW ONE and OLD ONE return to being themselves and go to bed.

The sound of a kookaburra heralds the morning.

THE BLACK SKIRT enters the dormitory and claps once.

The girls jump up and kneel beside their beds. They recite an abbreviated version of their morning prayer.

New One & **Old One** [*together*] In the name of her we pray. Amen.

THE BLACK SKIRT sends the children to work in the hot fields. She oversees their labour.

When THE BLACK SKIRT isn't looking, the children take a bite out of the fruit they are gathering.

A bell tolls and the children stop and rest.

NEW ONE spies two wooden 'Dolly' pegs on the washing line. She checks to see THE BLACK SKIRT isn't watching, then steals them.

NEW ONE shows the pegs to OLD ONE. She animates the two pegs, making them talk to each other. OLD ONE laughs.

The bell tolls again.

NEW ONE hides the pegs in her dress pocket and they hurry inside the orphanage.

Night falls.

The children kneel in prayer, then go to bed.

The voices of the spirit children fill the orphanage.

OLD ONE checks the corridors for signs of THE BLACK SKIRT. NEW ONE jumps out of her bed and begins another tale. She becomes MAGGIE, a child on the frontier, 1880.

Maggie Mother always said...

Mother Never wander off. The bush has beasts in it, wild things what will tear you limb from limb.

Maggie My home was a slab hut. My father cut the slabs from the trees. All day you could hear the ringin' of his axe beyond the creek. My father said...

Father All this is ours. You could walk three weeks and still not leave our land and I'll clear every inch of this bush before I'm dead. Of course...

Maggie   And he looked at me with disappointment.

Father   … I'll need the help of a son.

Maggie   So one day my mother had a baby that never cried. Father rode the horse a whole day to seek the help of neighbours, but by nightfall when he'd returned the babe had died. It's buried beyond in the bush, deep, deep in the earth so the beasts will not dig it up. Some nights I thought I heard it wailin', callin' for us to bring it back. Then I'd wake 'n think it was a bird. But my mother heard it too and was weepin' in her bed day and night. My father said…

Father   That's enough now. You want me to take you back to where I got you from? Is that what you want? To be locked up again with that convict scum?

Maggie   My mother's grief was silent after that. One morning I thought I would pick a posy to cheer my mother up. There were all colours of flowers in the bush if you walked far enough.

MAGGIE sings 'Ring a Rosie' as she wanders through the bush.

I never noticed the darkening of the sky nor the quiet 'til I stopped to pull a prickle from my dress. Then I could no longer hear the ringin' of my father's axe beyond the creek and I knew that I were lost. I called out, 'Help!' Only the birds called back. They found me, five days later, curled up in the hollow of a tree, my eyes shut like I was sleeping, but I was not.

THE BLACK SKIRT enters the dormitory. OLD ONE sees her and quickly returns to her bed.

NEW ONE, unaware of THE BLACK SKIRT's presence, releases the spirit of MAGGIE from the orphanage by flinging a sheet out into the air. She turns to discover THE BLACK SKIRT.

NEW ONE is frozen with terror.

THE BLACK SKIRT silently orders NEW ONE out of the dormitory. She leads her through the orphanage corridors and into the dark shower room. THE BLACK SKIRT abandons her there.

The sound of dripping water.

Above: Working in the fields.
Below: 'Never wander off.'

The voices of the spirit children fill the orphanage. Without OLD ONE, NEW ONE is paralysed by fear. She whimpers in the dark.

In the dormitory OLD ONE lights the candle with the box of matches she has hidden beneath her bed. She steals out of the room and goes in search of NEW ONE. The candle lights her way through the dark corridors of the orphanage.

OLD ONE finds NEW ONE crouched in the shower, shaking with fear and cold. OLD ONE whispers…

Old One Wanna tell another story?

NEW ONE shakes her head.

It'll hush them spirits, help 'em find their way in the dark.

NEW ONE nods. OLD ONE listens to the spirit voices.

NEW ONE becomes LUCY from the 1910s.

'The Lord smiling down…'

16

Lucy I was workin' for Mr and Mrs Reardon. I was the house girl,
see? I got let outta the orphanage early, got told by the sisters…

NEW ONE is still too terrified to join in.

Old One Come on, New One… I got told by the sisters…

NEW ONE relents and joins in, becoming the NUN.

Nun You have the Lord smiling down on your head, Lucy Hart.

Lucy I never saw it like that, 'cos that Lord he never would've
whipped me 'n he never would've made me work like I did. Each
mornin' I had to rise early before the sun, make sure the water
was boiled, eggs collected, cows were milked, horses brushed,
verandahs swept, breakfast cooked, dishes washed, the vegies
watered, the dogs fed and the pee pots emptied and scrubbed.
That's all before anyone else even got up. There was sewin' 'n
scrubbin' 'n dustin' 'n polishin' 'n washin' 'n brushin' 'n diggin' 'n
ploughin' 'n rakin' 'n choppin' 'n runnin' round like a chook with
its head cut off with every little order Mrs Reardon gave me in a
huff, 'til the sun went down. I'd just turned fifteen when that
war come. That's when we started knittin'. It was the year 1914.
Mrs Connell who they said was sewin' uniforms for soldiers back
in the Boer War asked Mrs Reardon could she spare me each
evenin'. So I was sent up the church hall after a day's hard, hot
work, me eyes nearly fallin' out of me head. Remember the first
time I saw ol' Mrs Connell…

Mrs Connell Do you know how to sew?

LUCY nods.

Those don't look like sewer's hands. Stick your thumb out.

LUCY puts her hands behind her back.

Stick your thumb out, girl, I'm going to test you.

LUCY refuses.

Stick your thumb out now or I'll be telling Mrs Reardon and you
know full well she'll whip you black and blue.

LUCY gives MRS CONNELL her thumb. She pricks it with a needle.

You're no sewer.

Above: 'Stick you thumb out, girl...'
Below: Listening to the wireless.

> *MRS CONNELL pricks her own thumb with the needle several times without flinching.*

Now that's a sewer's callous. Who do you think you're lying to but the Lord? Who do you think cares about your black tongue but our sweet Jesus? What did they teach you in that orphanage if not to sew? You'll never be married, I can see that. I can't trust you with the uniforms. I'll start you on the socks.

> *MRS CONNELL thrusts a pair of socks at LUCY.*

I find one hole in them soldier's socks, you'll start again, and you'll be here all night 'til you're done.

Lucy   Four years later when that war was over, the Reardons let me go. I walked out that front gate with no nothin'. No goodbyes, no thankyous, none of me wages from all them years, not even a cake or a biscuit to take with me where I was goin'. Where that was I didn't know, long as it weren't there, that's all I cared.

> *OLD ONE releases the spirit of LUCY from the orphanage by flinging a sheet out into the air.*
>
> *OLD ONE takes the candle and leads NEW ONE from the shower room, through the corridors, to their dormitory beds.*
>
> *The ghostly sound of a baby crying.*
>
> *THE BLACK SKIRT can be seen nursing what appears to be a baby in the distant corridors of the orphanage.*
>
> *The baby's crying fades.*
>
> *The children listen to the spirit voices.*
>
> *NEW ONE becomes IRIS, from the Great Depression, living in the inner city slums.*

Iris   I lived with me mum and me dad and me little brother in a little house in the big city. In the daytime, me brother 'n I played cricket in the street. At night we listened to the serials on the wireless. One day Dad came home late from work. He couldn't walk straight and he fell over and broke a milk bottle. He looked at us kids 'n started to cry…

Dad I lost me bloody job.

Iris The next day Mum went out lookin' for food and Dad was out lookin' for work. Me 'n me brother couldn't go to school 'cos we had no lunch. We were bored, so I played a dress-up game with a stray cat and me brother found a box of matches. The landlord came huffin' and puffin' at the door.

Landlord Little kids, little kids, let me come in.

Iris Not by the hair of our chinny-chin-chins.

Landlord Your mum 'n dad owe me one month's rent. Pay by tomorrow or get out. Rats is better renters than you lot.

Iris That day, Mum had to line up with lots of other mums to get flour, lard, soap, sugar and tea. On her way home through the dark city she was robbed by thieves and so she came home empty-handed. That night me brother was so hungry he couldn't sleep, so he played with his box of matches. First it started as a little flicker, licking the sheets of me brother's bed. Then it grew and grew and ate the whole house. Neighbours ran with buckets to try to put the fire out but it was too late. Only I escaped because the stray cat had woke me and led me out over the rooftops and down onto the street. A neighbour looked at me 'n said…

Neighbour Look at you, you're singed. All of your family is gone. You've got no one now, not a single soul in all the world. I can't look after you. There are places you can go. You'll be safe and happy there. Come along…

Iris So she packed me singed things in a little singed suitcase and took me to a place where little singed girls, who haven't a single soul in all the world, go.

NEW ONE releases the spirit of IRIS by flinging the sheet out into the air.

The spirits are quiet.

NEW ONE and OLD ONE return to their beds and fall asleep.

The sound of a kookaburra heralds the morning.

THE BLACK SKIRT enters the dormitory and claps once. The girls jump out of their beds and kneel on the floor in prayer.

New One & **Old One** [*together*] Amen.

> *THE BLACK SKIRT claps again. A macabre grooming ritual begins.*
> *NEW ONE and OLD ONE carefully brush THE BLACK SKIRT's hair*
> *and adjust her dress. Throughout this grooming ritual the*
> *children voice their true feelings in the following letters.*

Letter 1 Dear Mum and Dad, I don't like the orphanage. Some of the kids here don't have no parents. They're dead. Every day I look out at the gates to see if you're comin' to get me. How come you never come?

Letter 2 Dear Aunty, this a bad place, bad spirits 'n that. Soon as I can I'm gonna get outta here, gonna run away. Gonna find yer. I'll find yer.

Letter 3 Dear Mum, every night I sing the song you used to sing to me. I sing it in me sleep quiet so no one hears. Don't wanna be here, wanna be with you. Please come get me, please Mum…

Letter 4 Dear Dad, where are yer? Why don't yer come visit me, Dad? I don't like it here, wanna be with you. I be good, I promise.

Grooming The Black Skirt.

Won't ask no questions, won't eat much, won't break nothin', I swear. Yer won't have to belt me no more 'cos I be too good.

Letter 5 Dear Mum, what's a loose woman? That's what they told me yer was. Said they took me away from yer because yer was loose. Please don't be loose, Mum, wanna go home with yer.

Letter 6 Dear Dad, they told me you was dead. That you 'n me sister died in a car accident. I don't believe 'em. I hate 'em, wanna punch 'em in the stomach, wanna stab 'em with the pitchfork I gotta dig the paddock with.

Letter 7 Dear Someone, I don't wanna be here, wanna run away. I don't like the things they make me do, like brush the lady's hair. I don't wanna but I gotta. Jus' want someone to love me 'n come 'n get me 'n let me live with them. Hope you get this letter.

> *HARROLD HORROCKS, the Inspector of Orphanages, appears. He takes several letters from his coat pocket and begins to read them. The children appear and with an exaggerated cheeriness, recite the contents of these letters. Throughout, HORROCKS expresses his delight and satisfaction.*

Letter A Dear Mr Horrocks, Inspector of Orphanages, I am writing to tell you how grateful I am to you and to the State for taking care of me as I have no parents and am an orphan. Before, I was homeless, now I have shelter. Even if I don't have any blankets and am cold, I am grateful. Before, I was hungry, now I have food, even if it does have weevils in it, I am grateful. Before I was godless, now I am filled with the Holy Spirit, even if He does say I will burn in Hell, I am grateful. God bless you, Mr Horrocks, and God bless the Queen.

Letter B Dear Mr Horrocks, Inspector of Orphanages, I am so lucky to be an orphan. Other children have only one or two brothers and sisters but I have hundreds. Other children have only a backyard or a street to play in, but I have a whole farm to run and jump in. Other children do not get to learn fun things, like how to milk a cow, plough fields, scrub floors and build orphanages, like I do. Thank you, Mr Horrocks, and thank you to the State for looking after me.

Letter C Dear Mr Horrocks, I am writing to thank you for your generosity in looking after me. I have many friends at the

'Dear Mr Horrocks...'

orphanage. The Brothers like me very much. They are very, very kind to me. One Brother invites me into his room sometimes to see his stamp collection. Another Brother gives me lollies all the time. He puts the lollies in my pockets when no one is looking. Thank you, Mr Horrocks, and God bless you.

HARROLD HORROCKS dictates a letter.

Horrocks Dear Miss Emily Greenant, Governess, Golgotha Orphanage. As State-appointed Inspector of Orphanages, I am obliged to inspect your facility bi-annually. I shall be travelling by my chauffeured Rolls Royce and will be arriving at the orphanage at 10 a.m. sharp. I expect that preparations will be made for my inspection.

In preparation for HORROCKS' arrival, NEW ONE and OLD ONE begin a frenzied cleaning routine, scrubbing and sweeping the orphanage floors.

P.S. I look forward with much anticipation to sharing a morning tea with you, Miss Greenant, and to those ever-so-delicious savoury sausage fingers I had last time. I have dreamt about those fine fat fingers and I have woken on many a morning to find a patch of saliva on my pillow where my head has been, the wet reminder of my night's desires. Yours-in-service, Harrold Horrocks.

HARROLD HORROCKS arrives at the orphanage. He surveys his surroundings and continues to dictate his report.

On arrival at the orphanage I was met by a gaggle of bright-eyed laughing children, all clamouring to see this important visitor to their grounds.

The orphanage children greet HORROCKS with glum faces. NEW ONE opens the car door for him. He points his cane at her.

Hands off the car, you filthy twit.

HORROCKS continues to dictate his report…

I embraced each and every dear child most heartily…

HORROCKS waves the children away with his handkerchief.

Shoo. Shoo, all of you. Shoo. Oh, why won't you shoo?

HORROCKS approaches THE BLACK SKIRT.

Why, Miss Greenant…

He bows, takes her hand and gives it a saliva-drenched kiss.

A morning tea is presented to HORROCKS. He sits and fixes the tablecloth to his collar like a bib.

OLD ONE and NEW ONE appear in an endless parade, carrying plates of cake, slice, sausage fingers and pots of tea. HORROCKS gluts himself, washing it all down with great gulps of tea. As the crumbs fall from HORROCKS' plate, NEW ONE and OLD ONE hungrily lick them off the floor.

Oh, delicious. Yes. Oh, yes. Mmmm. Oh, wonderful, wonderful. Yes, another. Oh, and another one of those. Oh, yes, moist. Oh. What is that? Is that chocolate? I'll take one of those, oh yes, and another one of those. I did like those. Oh. Yes. Oh, good. Oh, that is good.

Harrold's morning tea.

So buttery, yes, melts in the mouth. Oh good, oh delicious. Oh, and another one. Yes. Mmmm. Oh. Yes. Yes. Oh, oh, oh.

Only one slice of cake is left on the plate. HORROCKS waves it away, he's had enough. The children's eyes widen at the possibility of enjoying the leftovers until HORROCKS has second thoughts. He grabs the last slice from the plate, wraps it in his handkerchief and stuffs it under his hat for later. He belches loudly, then dismisses the children with another wave of his handkerchief.

Shoo!

As the children take the morning tea away they chant grimly beneath their breath…

New One & **Old One** [*together*] Harrold Horrocks
Eats too much porridge,
He sucks his thumb
Then sticks it up his bum,
Mmmm, yum.

HORROCKS strikes his cane on the floor.

Horrocks Inspection!

The children quickly straighten their dresses and hair, then form an assembly line.

HORROCKS addresses members of the audience. He carries a small black book in which he records notes.

You step forward, what's your number? This child is too tall. Why are you so tall? Why is this child so tall? How old are you? Hmm? Speak up. No you're not. That's ridiculous. You are far too tall for ten. Are you a mutinous child? Do you think that you are above everyone else? Hmm? Then why are you growing so tall? You must stop it, stop it at once, I say. Miss Greenant, you must cease feeding this child. This child need grow no more 'til I say so. I should keep an eye on this one, Miss Greenant, history's rebels were all very tall people and this child has an eye of defiance in her.

HORROCKS moves along the assembly addressing another member of the audience.

You step forward. Why is your head so big? Look at it, everyone. This child has an enlarged head. That is a very serious condition. What have you been thinking that has made your head so big? You've been thinking sinful thoughts, haven't you? Your head is engorged with sinful thoughts. Your eyes are bulging with sin. You must take this child out of school, Miss Greenant, and put it to work all day in the fields. Hard, hot work will do it good. It will stop it thinking and its head will reduce slowly over time.

HORROCKS moves along the assembly again. He points his cane at OLD ONE.

S78. Step forward.

OLD ONE takes one step forward.

This child is dirty. Why are you so dirty?

Old One I'm not dirty.

Above: 'What's your number?'

Horrocks What?

Old One That's my colour, Sir.

Horrocks What? What?

Old One That's my colour, Sir. I'm Aboriginal, Sir.

Horrocks Nonsense. You do not wash yourself properly. Nonsense.
She is to scrub herself hard with a scrubbing brush all over, Miss
Greenant. We'll just see if we can't get that colour off you. We'll
just see about that. We can't have children looking like that.
Certainly not, certainly not. It's unacceptable, entirely
unacceptable.

> *HORROCKS thrusts a scrubbing brush at OLD ONE. She begins to
> scrub herself.*
>
> *HORROCKS strolls away with THE BLACK SKIRT.*
>
> *Night falls.*
>
> *OLD ONE is in the orphanage grounds still scrubbing her legs.
> NEW ONE goes to her and comforts her. She leads her inside the
> orphanage dormitory and to her bed. NEW ONE reaches out to
> touch OLD ONE's raw, scrubbed skin. She flinches with pain.*
>
> *NEW ONE has a great surprise to cheer OLD ONE up. She shows
> her the puppets she has made with the two 'Dolly' pegs she
> stole from the clothesline. One puppet is the likeness of
> HARROLD HORROCKS, the other THE BLACK SKIRT.*
>
> *The two girls play a rude game of mockery with the puppets.
> NEW ONE makes the HORROCKS puppet do a loud fart, etc…*
>
> *The game continues until it is cut short by the sound of THE
> BLACK SKIRT's keys jingling in the corridors.*
>
> *The girls jump into their beds.*
>
> *The voices of the spirit children fill the orphanage.*
>
> *NEW ONE becomes TOM, a boy from Manchester during World
> War Two.*

Above: 'She is to scrub herself hard...'
Below: 'Dolly' peg puppets.

Tom   Me father is dead. He was blown up by the Germans. Since me father was blown to pieces, me mother couldn't afford to feed us. Sometimes I would suck on me boot and pretend I was eatin' bacon. One day me mother dressed us in our Sund'y best and took us to see a fat man in a suit. The fat man said…

Fat Man   How would you two boys like to go on a holiday to Australia?

Tom   Yes please, yes please, we said.

Fat Man   There'll be lots of oranges and kangaroos. You can eat the oranges until you are sick and ride the kangaroos to school.

Tom   Yes please, yes please, we said. So me mother packed a suitcase.

TOM'S MOTHER weeps while she packs a suitcase.

We took the train to the seaside. Me brother cried because me mother was weepin', so I hit him on the head. He cried louder. There were hundreds of other children with suitcases gettin' on big boat too. I turned to me mother and said, 'Oy, aren't you comin' on boat?'

Tom playing war.

Tom's Mother I'm just goin' to buy you boys an ice cream.

TOM'S MOTHER leaves.

Tom We waited, but the boat sailed away to Australia. I never saw me mother again. The boat trip over was all right. I was sick and threw up in the sea. The fish would eat me sick. They seemed to like it very much. When we arrived, there was a welcomin' band with lots of people wavin' banners. No one was wavin' 'em at us, though. Then we got on a bus for many hours until we reached the orphanage, but the orphanage hadn't been built yet. For the first year we had to sleep in tents until we built our dormitory. That's where I grew up.

NEW ONE releases the spirit of TOM from the orphanage by flinging the sheet out into the air.

OLD ONE hears another spirit voice. OLD ONE becomes RUBY, an Aboriginal girl from the 1960s.

Listening to the spirits.

Ruby I grew up in Housin' Commission flats, way up on the 22nd floor. I lived there with me bubba sista' 'n me mum. Every night Mum hadda work. She was cleanin' toilets in the office blocks across the street. She'd say…

Mum You kids be good now. Don't cook nothin' 'n don't open the door to no one, yer hear?

Ruby We played hide 'n seek 'til we fell asleep. Then Mum'd come home smellin' of disinfectant 'n she'd put us kids to bed. One day, Welfare come knockin' on the door.

Mum You can tell that bloody mob by the way they knock. Quick, go hide.

Ruby When she open that door, Welfare lady standin' there all dressed up. Me 'n me bubba sista listenin' from the pantry where we were hidin'.

Welfare Mrs Murray?

Mum That's right.

Welfare I'd like to see your children please, Mrs Murray.

Mum Well, they're not here right now.

Ruby hiding in the pantry.

Welfare We've had complaints, Mrs Murray.

Mum What sort of complaints?

Welfare You've been leaving your children alone at night.

Mum Someone's gotta work, gotta earn the money, keep 'em fed. Their dad took off.

Welfare You should have thought about that before you had them, shouldn't you? I assure you, I'll be back.

Ruby Next night Mum goes off to work. She says to us kids...

Mum You kids be good, don't cook nuthin' 'n whatever yer do, don't answer the door to no one, yer hear?

Ruby That night me 'n me bubba sista was watchin' TV when we heard a knock on the door. It's that Welfare mob again. I tell me bubba sista, 'Hush now, be quiet. We'll go hide 'n we won't let 'em in.' But that Welfare mob, they got a key 'n they let themselves in. 'Hush now', I say to me lil' bubba sister, 'Hush now'. But she starts to cry, so I cover her mouth with me blanky. 'Hush now, hush.' But they find us hidin' in the pantry with the tins of baked beans. They took us away, that Welfare mob, gave us to another family, somewhere our mum'd never find us again.

OLD ONE releases the spirit of RUBY from the orphanage by flinging a sheet out into the air.

THE BLACK SKIRT appears in the dormitory. She discovers OLD ONE and NEW ONE out of their beds. She silently orders them out of the room. NEW ONE and OLD ONE look at each other and disobey. THE BLACK SKIRT chases after them with her scissors. They try to escape her, dodging and ducking her grasp. One of them seizes THE BLACK SKIRT from behind. She holds her while the other strips away THE BLACK SKIRT's dress, releasing the BUSH CHILD from the power of THE BLACK SKIRT. Once she is free, she quickly releases the others from the powers of their dresses.

The BUSH CHILDREN hear the ghostly crying of a baby. There is one story left to tell.

The CHILD who was THE BLACK SKIRT becomes the character of the BLACK SKIRT'S BABY from the 1890s.

Seizing The Black Skirt.

Baby I died before I was born. My mother lived in a fine house on a hill. All day she would play with her scissors and dolls, never speaking a word, for she was told by her aunt…

Aunt Children are to be seen and not heard.

Baby One day a visitor came. A tall gentleman with cancerous lips that he would lick as he leered. He gave my mother lessons in the parlour. Private and prickly. The tick-tock of the clock, barely a word between them. Then, a horrible movement. When my mother grew fat with me, she was silent and never spoke a word about the visitor, nor of the horrible movement for…

Aunt Children are to be seen and not heard.

Baby And so she bit on her lip when at dinner I kicked, and she stifled the beat of my heart with a cough. When the time came for me to be born, my mother could hide me no longer. She told her aunt in a hoarse whisper… The doctor came with his bag and his hat and he knocked on the door with a rat-a-tat-tat. He looked at my mother and he shook his head.

Doctor This baby will be born, but it will be born dead.

'Children are to be seen…'

Baby   So you see, I died before I was born. Still my mother will not release me. Forever she floats within these orphanage walls and I cannot stop my weeping.

The BUSH CHILDREN take a sheet and cast it to the wind, releasing the spirit of the BABY from the orphanage.

The ghostly cries of the baby cease.

The girls gather the clothes of THE BLACK SKIRT, NEW ONE and OLD ONE and burn them in the incinerator, releasing their spirits from the orphanage.

There is silence and peace in the orphanage grounds.

Night falls.

One of the children lights a candle and leads the way out of the orphanage and into the landscape.

THE END

Releasing the Baby's spirit.

Teachers' Notes

Written by Adrianne Jones and Michael Boyle

Edited by Dean Nottle

Thank you to Angela Betzien, Leticia Cáceres and Helen Strube

Produced by Education Queensland, Queensland Arts Council and Currency Press

INTRODUCTION

In the past ten years there has been increasing attention placed upon the treatment of children in the past and present, both here in Australia and internationally. The media has played an instrumental role in influencing and reflecting public opinion about the rights of the child and the role that adults play in protecting the young. Young people today need to consider how children have been treated in the past by institutions, government policies, and the community. It is important that students have an understanding of human rights issues so that they may reflect upon issues of access to power and rights and responsibilities in their own community and advocate for the protection of those rights.

Students should reflect upon the past and pose their own questions, and then transform knowledge into action. After investigations of their own, they should be able to communicate their findings and proposals, suggesting possible solutions to alleviate injustice.

These notes encourage Inquiry-based learning and Aesthetic learning to investigate an issue that really matters, requiring students to frame questions, consult a range of sources, and present their findings in a manner appropriate to audience and purpose. In order to accomplish this, teachers must adopt an inquiring frame of mind in their classroom and allow space for students to ask their own questions. Young people need to have opportunities to transform their knowledge of Social Justice through significant demonstrations.

BACKGROUND TO THE PLAY'S DEVELOPMENT

Real TV's vision is to produce new theatrical works that are innovative, physical and political. 'We attempt to interpret and articulate the dispossession, alienation and desperation of society, to tell the true stories of the underclass, stories that appear in few seconds' slots on the six o'clock news.' The artistic team consists of Angela Betzien (Writer), Leticia Cáceres (Director), Pete Goodwin (Composer), Tanja Bear (Designer) and Jodi Le Vesconte (Actor).

Children of the Black Skirt started its creative development as *The Orphanage Project*. It received support from Arts Queensland and

Queensland Arts Council to research orphanages. The second phase of creative development was supported by the Australia Council and Brisbane Powerhouse. The extended version of the *The Orphanage Project* script was programmed in 2003 at Queensland Theatre Company.

SUMMARY OF THE STORY

This story takes place in a mythical, timeless Australian orphanage. Two orphan children, Old One and New One, always wary of The Black Skirt (the cruel Governess who floats up and down the dormitory corridors, dangerously wielding her enormous scissors), tell terrible tales of other poor lost children to escape the reality of their own lives. The play delves into the history of Australia through the eyes of children, from convict times to early white occupation, to the vast era of the Stolen Generation to World War Two and beyond. Three actors create a highly theatrical, physical and visually spectacular gothic fairytale, as they slip in and out of different characters to tell us the tales of children from Australia's past.

THEMES, IDEAS AND PREOCCUPATIONS OF THE PLAY

- Transportation in early colonial Australia
- The lost child in Australian history
- The plight of orphans in Australia
- Abandonment
- Poverty and its effect on children
- The Stolen Generation
- Children being used as servants
- Child migration

HISTORICAL CONNECTIONS

- Colonial Australia
- Penal transportation
- The Depression
- The Stolen Generation
- Post-war immigration

PERFORMANCE STYLE OF THE PLAY

Children of the Black Skirt is a non-naturalistic piece of theatre recounting impressions left within the Australian consciousness concerning lost children. The piece benefits from abstracted or heightened movement and gesture to create a strong physical performance language. *Children of the Black Skirt* continues the gothic tradition and has its contemporary roots in Junk Opera (Shock Peter). The soundtrack is an integral part of the performance piece operating cinematically, like a film-score, to support and extend the dramatic action. Whilst the thematic territory explores the reality of child suffering in Australian orphanages, the piece has strong 'fairytale' imagery. Similarly, the use of nursery rhymes and rhymes underpin key ideas. The piece is strong in poetic symbolism making it suitable for the use of puppetry and shadow play.

DISCUSSION POINTS

The following points and sample questions can be used as a framework to stimulate inquiry into issues raised by the play *Children of the Black Skirt*:

1) Tuning In

What is power? In what ways may power be used/displayed?
What are human rights?
What are responsibilities?
What is power in art? What is power in history?

2) Preparing to Find Out

What do we know about the experiences of children in the play and what do we want to find out?
How do we investigate the experiences of children in Australia?

3) Finding Out

What have been the experiences of abandoned, lost and stolen children in Australia?
How have these stories been presented in different forms (art, historical sources)?
Why did these experiences occur?
What are the consequences of these experiences?

4) Sorting Out

What issues of power exist within the play and other stories and sources we have investigated?

Why have the experiences of children been presented in different ways?

How do we compare the power of art to tell us stories about orphans and the power of history to tell us stories about orphans?

5) Going Further

What elements of drama and dramatic conventions allow the experiences of children to be shared?

What attitudes towards children's rights are advocated in Australia and how can I advocate/prioritise these human rights issues?

What are society's responsibilities towards children?

What issues of power are involved?

6) Making Connections

How have my views on the lives of children changed?

Who are the future orphans of the world?

What is the relationship between power, rights and responsibilities?

7) Taking Action

What have I learnt about children's rights and the power over children?

What have I learnt about the craft of artistry and history to tell powerful stories?

How is power connected to truth?

How can I take action to express my ideas?

For what purpose can I take action?

How can we ensure that humans have access to power and yet ensure that power is not abused?

RESPONSIVE ACTIVITIES TO THE PLAY

Responding may take many forms. It is important that educators identify the nature of the knowledge gained from a work of art and encourage students to 'respond' to it by writing a review or by participating in discussion. These are valuable ways in which to respond, however students may also respond to a work of art by 'forming' and 'presenting' responses via poetry, drama, visual arts, PowerPoint, chat room correspondence, dance and so on. We often transform experiences into new experiences symbolically or metaphorically.

The aim and objective of these activities is to provide contexts for students to explore the themes and styles in the play and to allow them to reflect and define what childhood means to them.

ACTIVITY 1: THE WORLD OF THE CHARACTERS

Exercise A: Warm Up

Place the following rhyme on an overhead projector for students to read and recite in a circle. Add movement or gesture to emphasise meaning.

'Australia is a free land,
Free without a doubt,
If you haven't got a dinner,
You're free to go without.'

Exercise B: Character Sculptures

Students in pairs create two different sculptures that capture a character from the play that is most memorable for them. One student sculpts the other into their representation of the character. Share and deconstruct.

The main characters and storylines to consider are:

A chorus of nameless orphans
Old One
New One
Rosie (the laundry woman)
The Black Skirt
The cockney English boy, John
Lizzie (from Glasglow)
Mr Harold Horrocks (Inspector of Orphanages)
Maggie/family (the lost child scenario)
Lucy (the child servant)
The family who can't pay the rent and lose their house to a fire
The children who lose their father in the war and are sent to Australia
The children who eat the jam sandwiches and are taken from their mother

Exercise C: Character Building

Students in groups decide on one character and draw a large outline of the character on butcher's paper. On the inside of the drawing, the group writes key lines or feelings about the character. On the outside, the group writes key questions about the character. Ask the students to consider what the missing facts about the character are and devise an improvisation that supplies some missing information about that character. Improvisations could investigate the following situations:

- A scene that reveals details about the character before the context of the play.
- A scene that reveals a situation that could run alongside the play. (For example, a mother discussing with a friend or other family member the decision to send her child to an orphanage.)
- A scene that reveals what happens to a character after the play. (For example, what happens to Old One and New One or Lizzie the girl from Glasgow?)
- Present and discuss.

ACTIVITY 2: ABSTRACTION

Playwright Angela Betzien often asks actors to 'abstract' a piece of dramatic action. Students may explore this stylistic device using scenarios from the play. Experiment with the following process:

a) Students select an element – air, fire, water, earth or rain – and move around the room physicalising an aspect of that element. Students should initially concentrate on one part of the body and gradually let the whole body become that element. Add sound effects and play.

b) Students form groups and select one of the following scenarios from the play:

1. A parent at dinner telling the family he/she has lost their job.
2. A group of young orphans comforting each other in the middle of the night.
3. A young person being caught stealing or pickpocketing.
4. A group of children, migrating to Australia on a boat, looking at the Australian coastline.

Students realistically create a small scene that captures this situation. Once they have the scene complete all groups present to the class.

44

c) Each person then reconsiders the element they were playing with. They now add the essence of the element to their character. Some students may want to change their element to suit their character. The character becomes the element. Groups rehearse. Students are to exaggerate and overdo their element and see the effect. The scene is to look totally unrealistic. Present.

d) Students reflect on abstracting their characters by adding a small aspect of an element that is symbolic of their character. How can they layer in a movement or gesture that helps to create meaning in their performance? Do they add a slight tremor to an arm movement? How can they move their presentation from realism to a more stylised abstracted interpretation? Groups present.

e) Class to discuss the effects of abstraction in their own work and the way actors may approach the characters in *Children of the Black Skirt*.

ACTIVITY 3: EPITAPHS AND OBITUARIES

Students are to write an epitaph or obituary for the lost children in Australia. The class decides on minority groups that they might wish to focus on – children lost in the outback, the Stolen Generation, children lost during transportation.

ACTIVITY 4: WHAT IS A CHILD?

This extended activity allows students to anticipate and explore the key themes and style of *Children of the Black Skirt* and to investigate the key question 'What is a child?' These exercises are designed to cue students into the artform of the play and deepen the experience of reading the script or viewing a performance.

Exercise A: Warm up

Students are given the following line adapted from the opening scene, which they must memorise:

> 'Youse wanna story, one a them spirit stories?
> This is a story 'bout a lil' one come from far away.'

a) In pairs, students recite and repeat the line in turns to their partner as they walk around the room. Students should play with the vocalisation of the line and the acting style used.

b) Students then devise an ending to the line, 'I come from…' (Teacher to coach from the side that the line must reveal different places where children who live in Australia come from.)

c) Students rehearse the 'I come from…' lines with their created endings, then, in turn, present to the class.

Exercise B: Childhood

In groups, students design storyboards that chart images of children from colonial times through to now as depicted in the play. Teacher-led discussion should explore the following questions:

- What is a child?
- What age has been regarded as childhood throughout the ages?
- How have children been treated throughout the ages?
- What historical and economical conditions have affected the treatment of children?
- When would you have least liked to have been a child?
- Where and when have children been mistreated?
- How have attitudes to children changed?

Students reflect on the changing nature of childhood. The storyboards devised must cover at least four different eras and have a one-word title. Share.

Exercise C: Your Own Childhood

1) Students to improvise around the following theme: Imagine you are returning, after an absence, to your childhood bedroom as it was when you were seven or eight. Pretend you have travelled a long way before you open the door. Teacher narration from the side: 'How do you enter your old bedroom? What do you rediscover? Nothing has changed, each object is still in its place. You find all your old toys, your furniture, and your bed. The images from the past come alive again. Pick something from the room that captures what childhood means to you and take it back out the door with you.'

2) Students then all sit in a circle and in turn describe the object they have brought back from their childhood room. Debrief and discuss.

3) Teacher poses the question to the class, 'What is a child?' In groups students create a group sculpture which expresses a particular aspect of what childhood means to them and give it a title. Present. This is not a literal presentation.

Exercise D: Other Children

In groups students choose a picture from a magazine or newspaper that includes an image of a child. The group recreates the picture, each student assuming the position of someone or something in the picture. Encourage students to take on non-human parts of the pictures, eg. trees etc., to encourage non-realism. Each student generates 3-4 lines, which make it clear where he or she is and how he or she feels. Present and discuss.

ACTIVITY 5: POWER

In the following exercises students are provided with opportunities to become engaged with the topic, by ascertaining their initial curiosity about the topic, and then being allowed space to share and discuss their personal experience of the topic.

Focus questions:

What is power? In what ways may power be used/displayed?
What are human rights?
What are responsibilities?
What is power in art? What is power in history?

As a teaching consideration, it is suggested that students are given opportunity to record in their own 'think books' questions they have, thoughts they have, and feelings that emerge. It is also recommended that students be given access to a 'graffiti board' in the classroom where they can contribute feelings, thoughts and questions which emerge as a result of class activities.

Exercise A: Warm Up

Pied Piper Power – The teacher takes on the role of the almighty powerful Pied Piper who holds in his/her hands the most potent power of the universe (the Piper's hands and arms begin to shake with the awesome power and he/she begins to hum, slowly making it louder and louder).

Meanwhile the students who have been seated in a circle begin to hum also. The Pied Piper explains that he/she is going to send the power to other pipers, but warns that those pipers seated either side of the one holding the POWER will be shrivelled if they don't protect themselves by raising their hand and placing it on the cheek nearest to the person holding the POWER.

The POWER is passed by throwing it with great force to another whilst calling out their name. Noises accompany the passing of the power, such as *room ro shhooom.* Every time someone is shrivelled, he/she leaves the circle. The winners are the last two pipers.

Exercise B: Control

Discuss the following questions in relation to the play *Children of the Black Skirt*:

- Who was the one really in control during the story?
- Did this change as the story continued?
- What was it that allowed them to have control? (eg. conditions at the time, special powers, certain rights, particular responsibility?)
- Was this element of control used positively or negatively?
- Were the consequences positive or negative? How far reaching were these consequences?
- In what ways could these consequences have been managed or reduced?
- In what ways could this element of control have been minimised?
- In what ways does this element of control relate to concepts of power?

Exercise C: Definitions of Power I

Discuss 'Definitions of Power'. Some of the following definitions may be useful:

'Power is the capacity of individuals or institutions to achieve goals even if opposed by others.'

'Power may be defined as the production of intended effects.'

'Power is the ability to employ force.'

'For the assertion "A has power over B", we can substitute the assertion "A's behaviour causes B's behaviour".'

'My intuitive idea of power is something like this: A has power over B to the extent that he can get B to do something that B would not otherwise do.'

Power is 'the ability to satisfy one's wants through the control of preferences and/or opportunities.'

Power 'is the process of affecting policies of others with the help of (actual or threatened) severe deprivations for nonconformity with the policies intended.'

'Power is the ability to cause or prevent change.'

We can see that power has a few key characteristics:

- Power is relational; it requires at least two people or groups to carry it out;
- It depends on one's position in a social structure, so that power is allocated to individuals or groups depending on their structural location;
- It includes the ability to compel someone or a group of people to do what they otherwise might not, to convince others of the rightness of one's world view or plan of action, to will one's vision of the world into being, or to resist these things;
- And finally, it includes some measure of success – the successful exercise of power requires that one be successful in their plan of action.

Engage the students in discussion concerning how power is displayed in *Children of the Black Skirt*. Questions could include:

- Where were there examples of power in the story?
- In what ways were the definitions of power exhibited in the story?
- Was the power shared, transferred, commandeered, stolen? In what ways did this occur? To whom? With what effect?

Exercise D: Definitions of Power II

This exercise follows the discussions in Activity C above.

In pairs or small groups, students take on one of the definitions of power and create an improvisation which reflects that definition.

Before presenting to the class, the students should briefly explain the definition in their own words.

Class discussion should then centre around the differences between the definitions.

This activity is completed with students writing their own definition of 'power' which they record in notebooks.

Exercise E: Power Plays

Divide the class into pairs and allocate each pair a specific context for an improvised drama (eg. working in a laboratory, working in a hair salon, packing the car for a picnic). Then secretly give each student a specific aim that they have to achieve in their scene. An example could be:

- Context – Two scientists working in a laboratory.
- A: To get B to leave the room.
- B: To get A to allow B to participate in the new experiment.

Each student's aim should not be told to anyone else. The students are instructed to play their aim during the improvisation.

After each pair has played their scene, ask the audience to identify each person's aim. Engage the class in discussion:

- What ways did each person use to achieve their aim?
- To what extent was each person successful?
- How did each person use power to achieve their aim?
- Could they have achieved their aim in alternative ways?

Exercise F: Power Styles I

Introduce the concept of 'Power Styles' and discuss the various styles listed below, encouraging students to find examples of each:

Power Over (Hierarchic Style) Driven by status, elitism and entitlement. Will use fear and intimidation to achieve objectives.

Power Through (Competitive Style) Driven by systems, rules and competitiveness. Will use hard data and regulations to achieve objectives.

Power With (Collaborative Style) Driven by broad participation and shared decision-making. Will use negotiation and open confrontation to achieve objectives.

Power Against (Oppositional Style) Driven by a need to overthrow real or perceived oppressors. Will use chaos and subtle or overt sabotage to achieve objectives.

Power Created (Empathic Style) Driven by compassion and tolerance. Will use self-sacrifice and empathy to achieve objectives.

Each of these unique power styles uses control, decision-making, relationships, language and behaviours to achieve, influence or prevent the completion or attainment of desired goals.

Build upon the previous exercises by engaging students in discussion concerning power styles and how they are displayed in *Children of the Black Skirt.* Questions could include:

- What type of power styles are exhibited in the play?
- What evidence do you have to support your view?

Exercise G: Power Styles II

In pairs or small groups, students take on one of the power styles from the previous discussion and create an improvisation which demonstrates that style. Students are to consider:

- Gestures
- Body language
- Sounds
- Language used
- Use of space

Students present the scene and, following the performance, the class engages in an analysis of the improvisation. Questions could involve:

- Who had the power in the scene? For what purpose was it used? Was it negative or positive?
- How does language and sound reflect power?
- What gestures and body language were used to reflect power?
- Did the use of space influence power?
- Was there anyone in the scene without power? With less power? How did you know?
- Did the person without power or with less power allow it to happen? Could this person have used power themselves? In what way?

Exercise H: Role of Power

The word *power* has had a bad connotation for many years. It has received this reputation because most people associate the word with one side dominating or overpowering the other. Power can be defined as 'the ability to influence people or situations'. With this definition, power is neither good nor bad. It is the abuse of power that is bad.

Introduce 'The Role of Power' and discuss types of power and rules of power (see below).

Types of Power

Various types of power *can* influence outcomes. The word 'can' is emphasised because if you have power but don't use it, your power is of no value. Consider the following types of power and look for examples of each:

1. *Position*. Some measure of power is conferred based on one's formal position.

2. *Knowledge or expertise.* Knowledge in itself is not powerful; it is the application of knowledge that confers power.

3. *Character.* Individuals who are seen as trustworthy have power. They are perceived as trustworthy if they have a reputation for doing what they say they are going to do.

4. *Reward and punishment.* Those who are able to bestow rewards or perceived rewards hold power. Conversely, those who have the ability to create a negative outcome for the other party also have power.

5. *Behaviour style.* The most appropriate behavioural style is dependent on the situation. For example, if you are going through a divorce and want to maintain a good relationship with your spouse, you would use a supportive style. You gain real power from a knowledge of behaviour styles only if you can read a situation and adapt your style to it.

Rules of Power

Knowing the following rules of power comes in handy when entering into some form of negotiation with another person.

Rule #1: *Seldom does one side have all the power.*

Rule #2: *Power may be real or apparent.*

Rule #3: *Power exists only as long as it is accepted.*

Rule #4: *Power relationships can change over time.*

Rule #5: *In relationships, the side with the least commitment generally holds the most power.*

Exercise I

In small groups, students take on one of the types and rules of power and create an improvisation which demonstrates the type/rule. Make certain there is a distribution of types/rules to cover as much of the list as possible. Students present their scenes and, following each performance, the class analyses the improvisation. Questions could involve:

- How did one's position invoke power? What is the connection with the elements of tension and mood?
- How was knowledge used to invoke power? What types of knowledge were used?
- How did the person's character demonstrate power? For what purpose?

- How did the ability to distribute rewards and punishments imply power? How did this create tension?
- What behaviour exhibited/initiated power?
- Did one person have all the power? Was the power real or apparent?
- To what extent did the power exist only because it was allowed to exist?
- Did the power relationships change at all? In what way?

ACTIVITY 6: YOUR RIGHTS

Set up the room for a Commission of Inquiry into the orphanage in which *Children of the Black Skirt* is set. Students take on the roles of characters from the play as well as the Inquiry investigators.

The Commission should be set up formally with the aim of reaching arbitration between the authorities and the children who lived in the orphanage. In setting up the drama, consideration should be given to:

- the contributions of children to the family unit, including their rights, roles and responsibilities
- the children's contributions to orphanage life, including their rights, roles and responsibilities
- parents' contributions to the family unit, including their rights, roles and responsibilities
- the contributions of the authority figures from the play, including their rights, roles and responsibilities
- notions of what a family may be (nuclear, one parent, extended and so on)

The Inquiry should also make direct reference to some or all of the extracts from the Universal Declaration of Human Rights (1948) and the United Nations Convention on the Rights of the Child (1990) (see below).

Universal Declaration of Human Rights (1948)

- Article 3 – 'Everyone has the right to life, liberty and security of person.'
- Article 4 – 'No one shall be held in slavery or servitude; slavery and the slave trade shall be prohibited in all their forms.'
- Article 5 – 'No one shall be subjected to torture or to cruel, inhuman or degrading treatment or punishment.'

- Article 9 – 'No one shall be subjected to arbitrary arrest, detention or exile.'
- Article 13 – 'Everyone has the right to leave any country, including his own, and to return to his country.'

United Nations Convention on the Rights of a Child (1990)

- Article 3 – 'Parties undertake to ensure the child such protection and care as is necessary for his or her well being, taking into account the rights and duties of his or her parents, legal guardians, or other individuals legally responsible for him or her.'
- Article 9 – 'Parties shall ensure that a child shall not be separated from his or her parents against their will, except when competent authorities subject to judicial review determine, in accordance with applicable law and procedures, that such separation is necessary for the best interests of the child.'
- Article 11 – 'Parties shall take measures to combat the illicit transfer and non-return of children abroad.'
- Article 20 – 'A child temporarily or permanently deprived of his or her family environment, or in whose own best interests cannot be allowed to remain in that environment, shall be entitled to special protection and assistance provided by the State.'

Following the drama, reflect upon the action and allow for debriefing. Questions could include:

- What are human rights?
- Is every person entitled to basic human rights?
- What does it mean to guarantee rights in a convention?
- Should rights be guaranteed?
- Should rights be explicitly listed?
- How do you ensure that rights are respected?
- Do all people have a responsibility to ensure rights are respected?
- What is the connection between human rights and responsibilities?
- What power is needed to ensure that rights are respected?
- What power is needed to ensure that responsibilities are respected?

ACTIVITY 7: FINDING OUT ABOUT THE PAST

Students should be introduced to the following statements that have been made about the nature of art and the artist and history and the historian.

The Power of the Artist

'It is the function of the artist to evoke the experience of surprised recognition: to show the viewer what he knows but does not know that he knows.' (William S. Burroughs)

'Art is the stored honey of the human soul, gathered on wings of misery and travail.' (Theodore Dreiser)

'Art is a lie which makes us realise the truth.' (Pablo Picasso)

'The function of the artist is to disturb. His duty is to arouse the sleeper, to shake the complacent pillars of the world. He reminds the world of its dark ancestry, shows the world at its present, and points the way to its new birth. He makes uneasy the static, the set and the still.' (Donald Brittain)

'Faith is a way of seeing. And the function of the artist is to teach us how to see differently…' (Rev. Kent Miller)

'What was any art but a mould in which to imprison for a moment the shining elusive element which is life itself – life hurrying past us and running away, too strong to stop, too sweet to lose.' (Willa Cather)

'The function of the artist is to make the transcendent visible; to touch the soul in ways that match the soul; to enshrine beauty so that we may learn to see it; and to make where we live places of wonder.' (Joan Chittister)

The Power of the Historian

'History is something that never happened told by someone who wasn't there.' (Gomez de la Serna)

'The historian does simply not come in to replenish the gaps of memory. He constantly challenges even those memories that have survived intact.' (Yosef Hayim Yerushalmi)

'History is a myth we all agree to believe.' (Napolean)

'One must always maintain one's connection to the past and yet ceaselessly pull away from it. To remain in touch with the past requires a love of memory. To remain in touch with the past requires a constant imaginative effort.' (Gaston Bachelard)

'Any good history begins in strangeness. The past should not be comfortable. The past should not be a familiar echo of the present, for if it is familiar why revisit it? The past should be so strange that you wonder how you and people you know and love could come from such a time.' (Richard White)

'History is the witness that testifies to the passing of time; it illuminates reality, vitalises memory, provides guidance in daily life, and brings us tidings of antiquity.' (Marcus T. Cicero)

'The historian looks backward. In the end he also believes backward.' (Friedrich Nietzsche)

'In lifting the bonds of time and place, in freeing us from the tyranny of the present, history gives greater freedom and becomes the instrument enhancing liberty. Of all learned endeavours, the study of the past can be the most exciting, humanising, broadening – and hence the most liberating.' (Stephen Vaughn)

Exercise A: Responses

Discuss the meaning of each of the statements and what emotions they provoke.

The class then breaks into groups and each group prepares a short dramatic presentation (using words and physical action) which embodies the essence of one of the quotes.

A debriefing is then held to analyse the work. Questions should include:

- How were the emotional responses to the statements conveyed in performance?
- Did the performers find performance helped to bring out the emotional responses?
- What issues/questions emerged from the performances?
- How are these related to power, rights and responsibilities?

Exercise B: Discussion of Children's Rights

Ask the students:

- What issues concerning children's rights are occurring today? In our community? In the state? In our country? In the world?
- What issues concerning children's rights have occurred in our history?

- How are issues of power, human rights and responsibilities and the experiences of children connected?

Use the following headings below to brainstorm, as a class, and compile a data chart. Reflect upon the value of this exercise in helping clarify and resolve issues.

- Place
- Issue
- People Involved
- Possible Solutions
- Possible Consequences

Exercise C: Discussion of the Role of the Artist and the Historian

Brainstorm, as a class, possible sources from where the above information could be obtained. This could be recorded as a list or concept map. Then reflect upon each item to decide what information could be used by artists and historians respectively. Class discussion could also centre upon the nature of each source of information:

- How is the information presented in this source?
- Who decides how the information is presented?
- What does this say about how information/knowledge is valued?
- How do we decide if this source is reliable and accurate?
- Does this source present a certain viewpoint?
- What 'gaps and silences' could be contained within each source?
- What does this say about the problematic nature of sources?
- What does this say about the nature of knowledge?
- What are the responsibilities, if any, of the artist and historian in telling stories about our past?

ACTIVITY 8: FURTHER REFLECTIONS ON THE PLAY

Students in pairs retell the story of the play *Children of the Black Skirt*. They record key moments and turning points.

What sections surprised you or captivated you?

Which story most stayed with you after the play?

What does the play question? What questions does the play leave unanswered?

The play uses a variety of non-realistic devices. Make a list.

How are objects used to transform or tell stories?

The actors all play multiple roles, what devices can they use in the creation of roles?

Why does the play use nursery rhymes? What effect do they have?

Sound is used throughout the production to create meaning. Describe some of the sound effects and how they could be created.

ACTIVITY 9: IMAGES

In pairs or small groups, ask students to devise one of the following for the play, bearing in mind the style of theatre as well as the story, characters and setting:
- a publicity poster
- a stage set
- some costumes

ACTIVITY 10: IDEAS IN REVIEW

Set up a series of television interview improvisations in which one student, in role as an interviewer, interviews another who is in role as a member of the creative team behind *Children of the Black Skirt*. These roles may include the playwright, director, set designer, sound effects creator, costume designer, actor.

The interviewers should be encouraged to discuss the content of the play, its themes, style and research methods rather than simply a recounting of the story.

ACTIVITY 11: EXTENDED PROJECT ON CHILDREN'S RIGHTS

Individually or in small groups, students can devise a campaign for a particular audience which identifies a particular problem connected with children's rights, present ways to ensure that these rights are protected, and address how to achieve the balance of rights and responsibilities. This campaign could take a number of forms such as documentary drama, one-person show, written report, advertising campaign, extended analytical essay, film documentary, dance production, visual arts gallery display, etc.

SOME RESOURCES

Margaret Adamson, *Australian Women Through 200 Years.* Hong Kong: Kangaroo Press, 1988.

Peter Pierce, *The Country of Lost Children: An Australian Anxiety.* United Kingdom: Cambridge University Press, 1999.

Ann B. Tracy, *The Gothic Novel 1970-1830: Plot summaries and Index to Motifs.* Louisville: The University Press of Kentucky, 1981.

James Nixon, William McWhirter & John Pearn (eds.), *Poverty in Childhood.* Brisbane: Amphion Press, 1990.

PLAYWRIGHT

Angela Betzien was born in Rockhampton in 1978, and is currently based in Brisbane. She won the Queensland Theatre Company/Comalco Young Playwright's Award in 1994, 1995 and 1996. In 1999, Angela won the QTC/Courier Mail George Landen Dann award for her play *The Postcard*, and was appointed Writer-in-Residence at the Queensland Theatre Company. Her work has received several professional and independent productions, including *Dog Wins Lotto* (Queensland Theatre Company, 1997), *Playboy of the Working Class* (Queensland Theatre Company, 2001), *Princess of Suburbia* (Real TV, 2001), *The Kingswood Kids* (La Boite Theatre, 2002), *The Orphanage Project* (Queensland Theatre Company, 2003) and *Children of the Black Skirt* (Queensland Arts Council, 2003). Angela is also an independent teacher of writing, and a tutor at Queensland University of Technology. She is a member of the Queensland Theatre Company Board. Angela is currently working on a feature film adaptation of her play *Princess of Suburbia* and a new schools touring work.

DIRECTOR

Leticia Cáceres was born in Cordova, Argentina, and immigrated to Australia in 1991. She works in Brisbane as a director, dramaturg and acting teacher. Her directing credits include *Far Away* by Caryl Churchill (Queensland Theatre Company, 2004), *Something to Declare* by Michael Gurr (Actors for Refugees, 2004), *Children of the Black Skirt* (Queensland Arts Council, 2003, 2004), *The Orphanage Project* (Queensland Theatre Company, 2003), *The Kingswood Kids* (La Boite Theatre, 2002) and *Princess of Suburbia* (Real TV, 2001). Leticia has taught and directed at Queensland University of Technology and has collaborated with most theatre companies in Brisbane including, DeBASE Productions, Backbone Youth Arts, Rock and Roll Circus and Vena Cava. In 2004, Leticia held the position of Associate Director for Queensland Theatre Company.

COMPOSER and SOUND DESIGNER

Pete Goodwin is a classically trained electronic-music producer, live performer and DJ, as well as a composer and sound designer for theatre and film. He has worked under the guise of Brisbane-based production outfit 'smear' since 1998, and career highlights have included several independent CD releases, eight Queensland Theatre Company productions, all Real TV projects, several underground films, as well as nationwide multimedia performances at clubs, events and festivals (including Splendour in the Grass, Woodford Folk Festival and Queensland Biennial Festival of Music). Pete's relocation to Melbourne in 2005 will be the launch pad for his new music project and club night, 'red light disco'.

PRODUCER

Linda Page is currently working as the Youth and Education Manager of Queensland Theatre Company. She previously worked as the Theatre Administrator of Schonell Theatre and Theatre Manager of the Cement Box Theatre. Linda has been involved with numerous theatre companies in the last nine years including DeBase Productions, Cracka Theatre Troupe, Front Productions, Vegas Nerve Productions, Underground Productions and the Children's Festival at Woodford Folk Festival. Currently Linda is a producer for Real TV and a partner of Better Than Nuthin' Productions. She is on the advisory board for the Australian Drama Studies Centre and QUE Youth Theatre Inc., chair of Youth Arts Queensland's Transit Lounge Advisory Committee, on the steering committee for the Queensland Government's new framework for Education and the Arts and a judge for University of Queensland's Annual Drama Awards.